This is Alan Brownjohn's twelfth volume of poetry, including his *Collected Poems* – to be reissued by Enitharmon Press in 2006. The latest of his four novels is *A Funny Old Year*, and two classic drama translations (plays by Goethe and Corneille) have been staged in London theatres. As critic he currently reviews new verse for the *Sunday Times*, as well as poetry and fiction for other journals. He lives in Belsize Park, in north-west London.

Sheila and Gerry —

Alan Brownjohn

Alan Brownjohn

The Men
Around Her Bed

with every good wish!
9th October 2004

ENITHARMON PRESS

First published in 2004
by the Enitharmon Press
26B Caversham Road
London NW5 2DU

www.enitharmon.co.uk

Distributed in the UK by
Central Books
99 Wallis Road
London E9 5LN

Distributed in the USA and Canada
by Dufour Editions Inc.
PO Box 7, Chester Springs
PA 19425, USA

ISBN 1 904634 01 X

Enitharmon Press gratefully acknowledges the financial support of
Arts Council England, London.

British Library Cataloguing-in-Publication Data.
A catalogue record for this book is available
from the British Library.

Typeset in Caslon 540 by Servis Filmsetting Ltd
and printed in England by
Antony Rowe Ltd

For J. W. McC.
and i.m. D. C. G.

ACKNOWLEDGEMENTS

are due to the following, in which these poems or versions of them originally appeared: *Acumen, Agenda, Ambit, Chimera, HQ Poetry Magazine, In the Company of Poets* (Hearing Eye), *The Interpreter's House, London Magazine, New Humanist, Polka Dot Ceiling, Rialto, Rue Bella, the Shop, Times Literary Supplement, Waxwings from the House of Icarus.* 'Considering Grigson' first appeared in an anthology edited by Robin Healey celebrating the life and work of the poet and critic Geoffrey Grigson.

Three poems, 'Sea Change', 'Heroic Couplets' (addressed to 'Mr Simon Armitage') and 'Saturday Afternoon' formed part of a 2001-line poem in couplets written during the year 2000 to mark the correct date of the commencement of the third millennium: 31st December that year. All of the poem was composed extempore, without drafts or revisions, on a portable Olympia typewriter given to me by a friend. The extracts here appear unaltered.

CONTENTS

SEPTEMBER 1939

I walked into the garden afterwards:

Away up there the soft silver elephants

                    hovered   peculiarly

The wireless had gone over to
A band . . . Or a short feature?
Whichever, I didn't listen.

My mother listened on, half-listened on,
And was thinking, as she watched me from the window.
She told me that.

There was no one in the gardens on either side,
And I too thought: *It will be different now.*

The elephants' noses wrinkled in the breeze.

DIALOGUE OF THE BELIEVING GENTLEMAN
AND THE ATHEIST MAID

The Gentleman:

You crossed your legs and gave no reason why,
A moment ago. We were talking about the high

Implications of great art. I said 'They are religious',
A point of view you called 'preposterous'.

But I love the St Matthew Passion, I love the Mo-
na Lisa, both of which surely show

The power of a Higher Being. Then George Herbert – he
Who chastised wealth and pomp and vanity –

His work, for me, is intrinsic, and surely God
Decreed that it should exist? To me it's odd

To find some – Well, to find a girl like *you*
Who doesn't have any inkling of the true

Religiousness of Great Art. – And one more thought begs
An answer still: Why did you cross your legs?

The Maid:

In bed with you I could cure you of God;
But that wouldn't be to deprive you of Michelangelo's
David, or of the Resurrection
Symphony (so named), or of the Holy Sonnets.
It's 'God' I'm banishing, not the works of man
(Or woman, naturally.) – Including your Gerard Man-
ley Hopkins, great nature poet.
                            In bed we'd watch

10

Late dust coming in, as we'd leave a window open
To catch the pollen of the evolving flowers,
The dust from the roadworks, and from the crematoria
Cresting the bland peripheral hills of London
– Particles of our impermanency, but
Shot through with such infamy and pleasure, sent
Up by the tumult of the lovebeds where
Those who love love love Telemann as much.

SAYINGS OF THE UTOPIANS

In a neglected Utopian black-and-white film
Which dates from the nineteen-thirties, a beautiful
Young girl sits in a smart bright restaurant
To which she has been escorted by an old man.
He has a trim white beard and a cunning charm,
And one may assume he planned this carefully.
She had been alone in her cold, bare, silent room.
Here is warmth – and flowers, champagne – and a gypsy band.

Insofar as he is audible above
The deafening silken-shirted Utopian gypsies,
She is listening to him. He is saying, 'Every young woman
As beautiful as you should have three lovers:
A twenty-year-old for passion,
A forty-year-old for passion and experience,
And a sixty-year-old for passion, experience
– And wisdom' (thus the sub-titles render it).

She being a sharp-witted girl, as well
As a beautiful one, she rejoins, 'So which are *you?*'
He smiles, and is about to answer her question
With words of cunning charm that will change her future,
When the waiter interrupts them. He wants their order.
He is not the suave waiter you get in unreal films,
He is slow, and lethargic, and derives *no* interest
From the customers as a salve for his tedious task.

The timing has been ruined, the moment passes
And it can't be recovered. The old man does not seduce her,
She does not marry him and inherit millions
From his trade as an insurer; and launder them
Into a salon for young post-Dadaists.
To attain the ideal, first disperse all crude illusion.
The man who made this bitter-sweet comedy belonged
To the school of directors known as 'Utopian realists'.

CLOSED SONNET

Adequate reasons for the door left open:
The breeze all last night slowly working it open;
The leaving of it by someone – like this – open;
Or 'on the latch', thus intentionally open;
Which would have meant it was certainly open
For someone else to enter or return; though it is an open
Question exactly *when* they fixed it open,
Because no man or woman – or dog with open
Eye pretending sleep – was watching . . . But then – look – OPEN
It says on this side but CLOSED on the other, the open
-ness therefore being relative.
                              So, tell me, did you open
The page at this moment because you wanted some open
Air to enter your head? If so, you may open
At the next page now, describing a window. Open.

ANITA 1944

This refers again to Anita, she
Who was in an earlier poem. We
Never spoke, and I wrote it without praise
Of all her grace among the bygone boys

In those 1940s . . . But to-night I can see her bike,
On the easy pedals of which she mounted high
And rode away from the gang up Shorndean Street.
See it once more, and recall how I dreamed the sleek

Style of her body for a long long while
Before I would think of dreaming it in rhyme.
– Now there revisits, too, her pregnancy
By a legal husband, and the memory

Of her managing a pram with the aid
Of her practical mother as day by day they made
Their way up the same street, the Mum advising,
Anita in the fold, submitting, dying.

Awful to save her as a vision of
Fulfilment that needed nothing approaching love,
Just the dark fumblings of insomnia
When the maths wouldn't come out . . . Then I think of her

As perhaps alive? – Yes. Thankfully unaware
That in these memories she needs to share
Commemoration with the ack-ack sites
That kept me more awake on late June nights.

THANK YOU TRAILS

In the dream, I am heckling – or ignoring
By just talking through them – the commercials.

But what do I do when the 'trails' start advertising
My own future dreams! Coming SOON to all the screens!!?

– Like the one about the waitress in the old café
Where they stopped having waitresses thirty years ago

– She says, 'Come into the bookshop next door
At five thirty-five, I'll wait by the poetry shelf'

– Or the dream which allows me to keep an assignation
I denied myself one Polling Day before that

– When I'm knocking on hundreds of unresponsive doors
And foregoing the one door where I had a chance

– Or the even earlier one where I long to be
Like several envied sixth-form friends from school

– Fifty-five years ago, on the Geography Field Trip,
Described by one of them the following week

– Those dorms at the Centre where the two sexes fought
With pillows well on into the lovely small hours

– And the thought of those bushes he hadn't gone to with girls
But some had, and therein started their adult lives

– Which did not exactly work out like Geography Field Trips
In the wilds of Surrey; this dream was not retrievable

– And hardly produced with the same innocence
In films about later sixth-form generations

– With all the new unrecognised glamour faces
And soft-porn cuts from kissing to bed to clifftop

– And was therefore unique (and if I remembered the title
I'd see it when it came to the Finchley Phoenix)

– Oh thank you cinemas, oh thank you dreams,
Oh thank you trails I never want to talk through.

THE SECRET HATS

O dentists, no need for your Santa Hats in August!

If you cannot love me in a corporate hat . . . then I'll remove it

Post coitum no market for hats with feathers

The wedding pics in the locals: the frigid veils, the bridegrooms'
    trilbies past lust already

Near her traffic cushion, slow down for Tania raising her champagne
    – her paper hat out of the Pisces cracker

Who was it held open the twentieth swing door in succession? It has
    to be the gentleman in the black hat

Come out from that wall and put your lid on, post-box. Be a pillar of
    real communication

'My apologies!' – Thus the passenger in the hat, as he answers the
    mobile lent him against his wish

In fewer memories daily, Mariela's hat. All we ever saw above the
    wall as she strode into the Bursary

When he started his new religion what hat did he wear? The one
    that still means the worship of Wobbly Hats

The scattered ashes of my deerstalker friend as they plaster the
    hated ground elder

With the skewer, make more holes in your belt. Here you need *both*
    hands to hold your hat on in the wind

In the windy street, is the vendor's hat really holding down that pile of papers? Only with a stone inside

So why do they gather in coats and hats at the corner? To rename the street after a headgear guru

DYNASTY

The small thin ultimate glasses tuned with vermilion,
Or sometimes with ultramarine, trickled in
From the darkest bottles the cellar corners keep

– Our traditional postlude, stored and guarded
By a dynasty of pale and courteous faces
On whom the hereditary rights have been

Exceptionally bestowed; including the right to wield
The duster with the crest to catch away
The cobwebs of the intervening year,

And the ancient worn-out leather that gloves the hand
That twists the cork. *In piam memoriam*,
Or Absent Friends. Whatever. We toast the dead,

We toast the living, we toast each other.
We are nostalgic, so we toast Nostalgia!
It jogs old memories, it warms old spleens,

It outlasts the courteous, pale expressions
Of humble grandfather, father and son
As the dynasty passes the bomb from hand to hand.

DEATH AND GIRLS

You reached out a hoping
Hand, articulate in
Every finger, to
Another hand or to
An unpierced ear or to
A navy-blue tight waist.
Then you tried for some skin
Without a crucifix
On the white space below
The neck above those, oh
Those . . . And it reached nothing.
And it never did then,
That being in nineteen
Forty-nine.
         When the brain
No longer moves the hand,
Is it more bearable
When it's past all hope, past
Even the hope of touch?
With all it feels for quite
Incontestably gone
Out of reach? *Out of reach?*

VOCATIONAL

It's black-and-white and jumps, and the sound-track drones
With out-of-date experience. They all speak
In ancient Yorkshire accents, broad flat tones
It took them not much practice to get right.
The band goes slowly through an old-world song.

Later a boy leaves a girl at a garden gate
With a good-night kiss she refuses to prolong.
'Did you see those good-looking chaps in the hall tonight?
One asked me to dance. He asked Jean for a date!
They were from the *colliery*.'
                                    This was the idea:

That men were needed to work six days a week
Down the mines, so miners got the girls. But here,
In our new world, girls dance upside down while a guy
In shades raps, growls and smirks, and rests
His hands on a car wheel. Then the girls deny

Gravity no longer, and resume their breasts
The right way up. Some casino you've never found
Is where they'll all finish. Life means: to shirk
Life for its vanities, you have to shave
With a VIREX razor, and not slave underground.

Long before Love and Music came love and work.
The girls can always be got to sing and dance
For the right kind of job, or that is what
The publicity says will happen . . .
                                    Now that he has
(With all the jumping screens turned off) his chance

To address the wordface in the dark, and scrape
At its enduring surface, seriously
Trying to work out how such things take shape,
Will he know why, at the window, all he can see
Is one girl walk past whom he hasn't got?

THE FAITH FAIR

My Dad was rather short, and he carried me
On his shoulders so I could tell him everything.
'Watch the Bull Courting Europa!' The crowd was dense,

But I did my best to describe things. The second day
Was 'The Gentlemanly Swan Meets the Lovely Leda!'
Same man, same woman, just the costumes different.

I told Dad that, but he wanted to come back
For the third day as well: 'Guaranteed Appearance
Of the Holy Ghost, First Time Here. Feed Him Yourself!'

The crowd was thicker than ever, the man wore
Feathers as for the swan, but fewer now.
I had to tell my Dad that the woman looked

Just as gratified, but that the show lacked spirit.

SESTINA: 1950

(for Dennis Saunders)

I am writing this down on a late June evening
In the future we talked about. It's midsummer,
Now as then. The air is still humid, the treetop colours
Are the same as they were at that time, untouched
By any change time might have made. The moment
Feels the same as when we stepped out on the terrace

Fifty years ago, for air, and looked back in from that terrace
At our past, deliberately. For me, the present evening
Has stopped at that sudden recall of the moment:
Saunders closes the glass door on our Midsummer
Party and the dancing, and we both stand there, untouched
By time. I feel it all as I did then, its colours,

Lamps and music – not knowing the colours
Of another world were waiting beyond the terrace
Den and I were standing on, a somewhere untouched
By our youthful energies. That those evening
Sounds of seventy-eights on that midsummer
Night of our last week at school are ending at that moment

We do not understand, it does not seem a moment
For growing that much older in. We look at the colours
Back inside the room, hear the sounds of our midsummer,
And find them sufficient; from that redbrick terrace
They appear to stretch out beyond our evening
And claim all the growing darkness, a place untouched

And ready for their brightness!
                              Our night could not stay untouched
For long. There would come for each of us some moment
To alter everything in less than an evening,
And disclose another future. The dancing colours
Inside the room called us back, but the dusk of the terrace
Predicted (we did not know) a dark to cancel midsummer,

And forestall our inheritance of *any* midsummer.
We could not see, we who were so untouched
By experience, that we stepped away from that terrace
As onto a mountain ledge not long after that moment,
Even though the air felt gentle and the comforting colours
Back there in the room seemed immune to the darkening evening.

Our midsummer became dangerous at that moment.
Such seasons don't stay untouched, and keep the same colours.
Our futures required us on the terrace of that last evening.

BLANK PAGE BETWEEN

Like an unexpected No Man's Time between fear
And some activity dispelling fear

Like a joyful second known on a short walk
To the Post Office or the Co-op, or like a talk

On a telephone suddenly turning
Much happier when a repeated joke is earning

An old friend's laughter, as if he'd never
Heard it before (he being ever-

polite and sensitive, infallibly there
Any day or place, always ready to outstare

The gaze of the passing Princess from her carriage,
Offering death and marketing it as marriage).

CONSIDERING GRIGSON

Impatient about large things, he loved small,
A tall man who was thought to be easily angered,
But turned out gentle to meet.
                                    The pebbles on the beach,
The words on the chimney breast, the hedgerow
Flowers he lived long enough still to find,
He loved those.
                        The vanity, the inflated fame,
The poetry elbowed to the front of the little crowd,
The empty vessel's charisma
                                    – He hated them.
What he did all his life was say Look, Look,
When the world was forcing its own pictures on our eyes,
But remember: *Think* while you look.
                                    This was 'serious'
Intelligence (to use a usage he would not
Have liked) . . . But he could also be outrageous.
– Am I right to think:
                        that *in the puritan nineteen-fifties*,
He persuaded a producer to induce an actor
To say it fast, and with no one writing to complain,
The small word 'cunt' was first broadcast? On the Third?

THE ALCOHOL

The two modes: first the dull and logical
That belongs to morning; and then the second,
The desirable tinted mode of early evening,
Where you smile and you wonder . . . After all,
Was that penny-plain other one really so useful?
Or just a flat version of what has come later on,
A mode that grasps and simplifies whatever
It can touch? And whatever it can't counts as not
Worth touching anyway?
                              You can walk out on its ice
Forgetting its thinness, and even allow some tears
Of what's called 'generous emotion' to drop
And turn into ice-sculptures. And then there is
A third mode, if or when the ice –

LIAISON AND CARROLL

I

Here is a corridor cleared to become
A narrowing perspective of doors fixed open
Going forward to a culmination where the sun,
Dropping down through skylights, points to an obvious answer.
– But you know rather well that there is a problem:
There's an apprehension of certain events about
To happen all over again, and it does not please you.

Yet you walk it like a lord of grand indoor distances
Who can conjure up unseen respectful glances
From a hundred fallen-silent side-offices
– Until at the sunlit end, and its special room
With the fruit bowl finely replenished alongside
The Book of Dreams rectangularly open
At Name and Signature and Comments, you turn back.

II

She said, 'Has one as young as me
    Done this with you before?'
He said, 'If you would quietly close
    The estuary door,

'I shall relate a circumstance
    I'd rather not explain
Within two miles of anyone
    Who caught the Oxford train.

'It was an hour of deepest dark
    One sunny afternoon,
I pleaded with her, "No, not yet,"
    But she was saying, "Soon!"

29

'We lay below the celery hedge,
    She gripped me hard and wept,
"You made a hidden vow to me
    An oyster would have *kept!*"

'I said, "That was not me but you,
    And one vow is absurd,
And are you sure you did not make
    A second and a third?

"We pledged to keep them secret so
    That each might know the facts
Who questions us, infers, or hints
    Or adds up and subtracts?"

'I was her next, she was my last,
    The others said the same,
But others still just looked away
    Or played a safer game.

'And when we stopped, to our relief
    We had not done the worst.
– It was her fortieth birthday and
    Next day my thirty-first.'

THROUGH GLASS

I have gone by too quickly for only
a second sharply catching the two men
through two walls of glass the bus window's
and the café's where they sit in a fierce crouch
facing each other with strip light falling
across their small glass cups as if there were
still something in them while one of the two
is lifting his own with hope in the silence of
their defeated staring down at a table top
itself made of glass but without a pattern
or anything underneath it to stare out
while outside the feet go patrolling past
at dawn and in twilight perpetually
towards what the two think close in on their short lives
like punctuation marks: satisfactions.

THE GHOSTLY REGIONS

There are some left, some ghostly, ghastly regions
   Crossed by stale stopping trains where many seats
Are occupied by pale purposeless poor, and by silent
   Unremembered girls found later dismembered
By Senior Citizens sauntering back from the bingo
   In black bags in alleyways, or shallowly buried
In woodland frequented frequently by rapists
   Descended from decent cheerful chapelgoers.

One such was Melissa, meticulous in arithmetic, always
   Achieving praise for perfection when she presented sums
To the lovely Miss Wolfenden, weary at the teacher's task.
   And she spelt superbly, and her geography projects
Were never less than neat, and chastely coloured.
   She would settle down to be, and be seen to be,
A suitable silent spouse for a friend in her form,
   It being obvious there was no better option.

It was not as if she was utterly unaware
   Of her elder brother's brackish activities.
Insofar as she thought, she thought them unimportant.
   So her parents placed her, they put her down with a frown
As a plain, private girl . . . she'd come to no horrible harm.
   Not for her the coarse canal, near that banal
Locality called 'the Loveys' where local lovers
   Would go and be mocked at by prurient-curious children . . .

– And one day Melissa was found – staying late in the Library
   Rejecting the ruffian who avidly approached her
And rested a rigid hand on her shapely shoulder
   Suggesting a droll little stroll in the brisk bright weather
To the worst of the hairy havens where all hope withered,
   – Found with eyes down on Emily Dickinson, read with dread
For the first timely time – seized and studied,
   To shake herself fatefully free of that breathing shadow.

SONNET FROM THE UTOPIAN

The Glitch who live in Paronomasia
Suffer for that. As do the Latitudini
Under the Puritanians, whose Holy Days are
All seven, except for Tuesday.
                  And you should pity
The poor Puritanians in the Glitchian part
Of Latitudinaria, who have to bear
Contempt from both peoples, and practise their art
In secret and in solitude.
              And, oh despair,
Despair, you gentle Arcadians! Loathed by them all
For your emphasis on Mortality, *Et in
Arcadia ego*, etc.
           We Utopians shield
Ourselves from such ridiculous feuds, and shall
Stay safe as chameleons are safe, set in
Strange ways of changing colours and being concealed.

A DAY IN 1966

I was ambling up from the Lower Annexe
– As distinct from the 'Upper' or 'First' Annexe built
With the flood of funding that also appointed me –
And along the covered uphill walkway between
The Library and the new Biology Lab
When I saw, as I passed the Senior Kitchen window,
The girl with her hair on fire.

The Principal Lecturer in Cookery, the President
Of the Junior Common Room, the Netball
Vice-Secretary and various beautiful
Young girl – or 'woman' – students (as we were starting
To describe them) were just standing round and looking
– That being the one-tenth second in which
They had heard the howl, and turned, and seen

But hadn't moved. Oh god, Jane's hair,
Is a scream of flame – I have to reach –
Reach her – All they do is stand and watch.
And then I am pushing through the heavy outer door
Of the Senior Kitchen, and through the lobby where
The coats are left, and Jane's howling head
Is being smothered in a coarse white apron

Grabbed from a proximate peg by Victoria
At the Principal Lecturer's shouted instruction.
– Out of which Jane's face comes finally
In a sudden trembling rictus of distress
I have seen before, but might not say when or why,
And with an indrawn Oh of astonishment
Staring at me. And what am I doing there?

TOP DOWN

Roof Terrace: There are white mountains;
And cranes, waiting by the new
Cultural Centre.

Ninth Floor: Nominal armchairs . . .
Well you could use them of course,
If the lift was late.

Eighth Floor: I'm telling my life
To last year's blonde chambermaid,
In stupid detail.

Seventh Floor: Atmosphere peaceful
– Until the lift opens and
I get, *Good morning!*

Sixth Floor: I'm a non-smoker
In this 'Smoking Zone'. Why should
The air be this clear?

Fifth Floor: In an old armchair
An old person sleeps. Well, say
An old lady, yes?

Fourth Floor: (She'd opened her eyes
And needed the lift, I had
To help her, so make

Fourth Floor: A second attempt):
Red-cloaked cleaners sing, and scour
A shining new space.

Third Floor: I touch a drooping
Cactus. It droops farther still.
Must I feel guilty?

Second Floor: My own floor, with three
                 Christian tracts on the table.
                 Not mine. Nobody's.

First Floor: The lift opens on
                 A depiction of my head,
                 Top half: hair, eyes, nose.

Mezzanine: These days no chairs. Just
                 An old pool table, ripped at
                 The starting spot. Life.

Ground Floor: I sink on a couch.
                 Who else would sink on a couch
                 Except haikuphiles?

FIVE RECOLLECTIONS

(for, and about, Peter Porter)

1

It was the thank god not 'youthful' nineteen-fifties,
Before the Teenage Consumer; but even so
It was hard to imagine being thirty. 'This is
My first year of middle age,' a writer I know
Was saying about achieving twenty-nine . . .
One night, as we left the Stockwell basement room
And scanned the next week's songsheets in the shine
From the concrete streetlamps, seven rockers with a zoom
Of gleaming new machines buzzed and bellowed
Past along the dark street; and were younger
Even than we were. 'Thom Gunn's gang
Have followed us here,' you decided.

2

       Our shared anger
I recall next, some time in (as they now require)
Our 'thirty-somethings'. We were waiting
Nervously, to read at the Royal Court, while a dire
Contemporary went on and on orating,
Overrunning. 'I've got the Christ-shits!' you declared
In the shabby wings darkness; and I heard a liquid noise
Of something hitting the boards, and hardly dared
To think what it was – in fact nothing worse
Than your g and t, spilt from a trembling hand.
But at last the man stopped, and you finally strode out
To the confident footlights and took your stand
On Sydney Cove and Rilke. Without any doubt
Your hilarious, erudite, impeccable
Act was the best that night.

3

Christmas! the very
Word is like a kick in the most vulnerable
Areas of consciousness. And, a scary
Prospect, the TA14 was (I could hear)
Making dangerous noises, an elegant intention
Gone for nothing. I was alone, in a year
All connections seemed in temporary suspension;
So to get invited over to Cleveland Square
Was a better prospect than I could have dreamt.
I drove across there on a crest of rare
Optimism, stressed out and unkempt
But hoping that I could forget it all.
Which I did, with Bruckner's Ninth and what I'd just bought:
Stravinsky's modern take on a Bach chorale:
Von Himmel Hoch, his variations on the same.
I also recall you on the life of the alligator
As 'the new business cosmology, the way the game
Will be played in the seventies'. Two days later
The Alvis finally cracked up on the A4.

4

The nineteen-seventies came. By then, the zeitgeist
Was worse still. When asked – 'I wouldn't open my door
To a knock on a stormy night to: Jesus Christ
As shown in *The Light of the World*, King Lear
Of course, or –' I forget the third. Your terse reply
Helped me slog on through each degrading year
Of the nineteen-eighties, with their vast supply
Of trios on which to slam the door very hard.
Cruel? But not serious; though I learnt to know
That this was the kind of game one always played
With tact and caution – best always not to show
Too much contempt of icons, be too satiric:
Some people think that Elton John is *singing*,
Some can sit straight-faced through a Bob Dylan lyric.

I know I *can* see either of us flinging
Our generous front doors open, unsuspicious,
Kind, and hospitable to literally any
Example of humanity, real or fictitious:
'Come in, Sir David . . . Lisa, I'm honoured! – *Tony!*'

5

And when I am complained at for making light
Of what I maintain isn't worth the sweat –
Costume serials switched off, rock reviews binned on sight –
Sometimes going so far as to say 'Forget
The lower opuses of even the best',
I cite to myself my emphatic conclusion –
'You set your sights higher than practically all the rest' –
On that early-nineties night at the High Commission,
I had sat there looking round without surprise
At an audience with its share of famous faces
Grounded firmly on the shores of compromise
(There I go again!) and had thought, 'The firm traces
Your two feet leave have invariably been
Set in the one camp: with those for whom an art
Mattered more than life, almost, yet are always seen
By those valuing life to have played a large part
In making it more liveable.'
                                    Our twenty-first
Century may not be much more improving
Than the one we still inhabit, surely the worst
So far for the wide scope of cold, unloving
Acts done in the name of tribe, or god, or bank
– Or focus group these days – whatever will contribute
Celebrity, power or profit. Listing those I thank
For upsizing art and life, I soon arrive
At your name; and your honest feet now turned
Towards an eighth decade, irrevocably come
Ten months before we all go, praised or spurned,
Up the Shit Creek of the Millennium.

ON THE TELEVISION

They come at you getting larger all the time,
The vast obscurities; and cloudier, even though
You can tell those are lips and eyes and cease
To look.
           Do we need to live with endless
Coloured grains that won't respond to talk or touch?

Won't respond any more than the eyes and lips of lovers,
With their breathless dotted faces closing in
Wanting love you can't provide?
                       I'm told there is
A handset to switch them off with . . . Can't I tell it
From an electric razor, or a mobile phone?

THE PRESENTATION

She becomes aware of the men around her bed
– The four of them edging up with blue,
Mauve, red and yellow bunches – when one has said,
As she opens her eyes and is plainly seeing them,
'There you go, young woman, all for you
With our love and thanks. Get well, Deb – soon!'

                                              The hem

Of the scarlet curtain doesn't keep out the sun
At half-past five; so she wants it pulled, and that
Is done by one. One unwraps the flowers. And one
Goes for scissors to do surgery on the stalks.
Then the cheerfullest, the fourth, in his bobble hat,
Leans down to kiss her, after which he walks

Away up the ward to fetch vases so that each
Can fill and arrange a vase and lodge it there
On her locker, brightly. Then they smile and reach
A hand out, one by one, to her warm long hand,
And stand back to attention, a rigid pair
On either side of her.

                       We can understand

How they all thought this could have been a funeral
They'd come to say goodbye at – but oh, was not –
With the flowers and that; then it sneakily came to all,
And at the same moment, that this was about Life
– Which Deb was for enhancing . . . And so what,
If every man there had a job, and wife?

Hell, for an hour they'd switched their meters off.

SONNET: HER HUSBAND

The surgeon spends his weekdays saving bodies.
On some week-ends he climbs into his car
(Leaving his wife behind) and among the trees
Of a particular forest fairly far

From hospital and home, he tracks and shoots
Wild boars. The hunters hire men in black boots
To haul away the bodies, and they expect
To have to bury most of them . . .

                                        Am I correct

To think his colleagues disapprove, concerned –
As he is – with ideas of saving life?
No, I am not. But it's true about his wife.

She can't see how his weekdays should have earned
This kind of leisure, taken with no distress.
– She and I think he is a moral mess.

TRADE-IN

I sit in what they call a 'screen' adoring
The colonisation of death by luxury:
The thousand-dollar hair will last for ever,
The stretch limousine drives on even though 'a storm
Of fire engulfs it', as the voice-over says
In the TV report. I survive, and watch
Two rescuers run along a girder, inventions
The world will validate quite soon enough.
The drinks in the cabinet will go on even longer,
They are like the divorces, called on at any time
To renew the life the long-lost marriages
Were once contracted to renew.
                              But wait – Look – Now –
It's the end at last. Here's the sunset, creeping us out
To darkness over the sea while the credits
For Platonic Productions roll up in pure gold,
An everlasting list of timeless names.
I get up with my own name and feel mortal
Trading all this in for the street outside.

TESTAMENTARY

I

I sit discussing notional death, stared down
By rows of unread tomes and the tall frown
Of the lawyer who owns all those titles in legal gold.
He's just thought to ask: *Now, if I might be so bold*
– If you went under a bus today, seeing that you
Haven't changed this clause, would you want your residue
To go to Flicky? . . . I pause . . . *Well, tell me in due course.*
– And it seems to me that things might get even worse
If more chance deaths came to cancel all this out,
Not just my own, but Flicky's . . . Even, no doubt
My interlocutor's – any of us could meet
Our ultimate bus on the uncongested street

Downstairs; on which, in a dream that very night,
I stand half-dazed in a curious pale light
And gaze across the road at a cemetery
Going on and on from his office right to the sea:
Cross on white cross on unmarked plain white cross,
And none of them due to an accidental bus.
At the seaside, my lawyer and a woman friend
– Christ, it's *Flicky*! – swim towards me from out near the end
Of the pier, transformed and harmless. And I feel fine,
Now I see that none of my residue can be theirs,
Merman and mermaid having no legal heirs.

II

The two sly faces stare across the restaurant
In the direction of a third, thinking they see
Flicky sitting there – what a great coincidence!
The third has no idea why especially she

Is being gazed at, it's one of her paranoid days:
The sun rose late for her alone, lunch is
Served horribly because they knew she was coming.
And then, in the freezing dusk, her toboggan crunches

On a snow-covered rock . . . At Reception, a girl
Who has slept with the casino manager and can map
The unlucky ones a mile off, induces her to
The tables out of loyalty to her chap

– And she goes, and loses.
                                        But under the same rock
Is gold, and under the gold a codicil
By some circuitous circumstance providing
For her to *inherit* this land. And so she will

Be wealthy through a careless codicil
When the casino manager dies in the girl's bed:
He has unknowingly willed his residue
To this unknown distant cousin, not having said

Some words to his lawyer to prevent all that.
                                                    It would
Be wonderful, the two faces are assuming,
If that *were* Flicky and not just her look-alike.
– They should stop, and remember what's always looming

To alter lives; and not upset with their staring
This one who will board a train of grand events.
She can see them staring, now, so she looks away
And picks at her food with wronged indifference.

SEA-CHANGE

I saw a sea-change that came suddenly,
As they are not supposed to. In the three
Miles or so between Brancaster and where
The North Sea becomes the Wash, the large share
The saltmarsh takes of the landscape finishes
Abruptly in dunes and reeds, diminishes
To mud and sand behind the rising banks
Which keep the ocean back. Beyond them, ranks
Of breakwaters split the waves, cargoes of rocks
Held together by wire meshes. There the sea knocks
And goes away answered and forbidden, sent
Back to the hectares of its own element.
In stretches of this coast it stays like that,
The wind-wrought beach surviving vast and flat,
Not drawn away by ravagements of tide.
This is a place where sour soil has defied
Water – and grown. Because dark grass has spread
Where distant sea has left the beach for dead,
And samphire, growing here in shifting mud,
Not in high cliff-face crevices, can bud
And flourish, threaded with salt but green,
A nominal reclamation; though, where the sea has been
It can come back. Incautious man may find
Sea-change does not exclude a change of mind.

AT 5.30

(for Peter Scupham)

they are leaving
The consultant's recommendations
And the boss's interpretations.

It's all about
The carefreeness of the body having
The evening before it, the day behind,

Though still the consultant's bending
Over his computer, sending
Them off next day like ball-bearings

Up the groove of the machine
To start the helpless casual roll
Down the slope which lights no scores.

There's really a regress in their going
From this hope to home; but they feel,
At evading consultant and boss,

No dread of betraying them, and no vast
Sense of loss, just a sort
Of residual guilt felt faintly.

A sort.

TALKING ANIMALS

Why don't we lie here and make up
New animals, I said to her;

Not thinking that – not consciously –
It was a blatant metaphor.

She left me. And she went and had
Liaison with another chap,

Which in the course of thirteen years
Put various creatures on the map

Who, yes, were new, and animals,
But not the sort *I* would invent . . .

– One's dead, one's rich, and one's still at
The University of Kent.

HEROIC COUPLETS

On Being About to Commence Reading
Killing Time
by Mr Simon Armitage
(in Transylvania)

I feel compelled to say something in rhyme
Before I start Armitage's *Killing Time*:
Did he *have* to do it, write for t'old folks at t'Dome?
Was it his destiny, fixed in his genome,
That my young Gregory prizewinner should come
To bow down to the New Millennium
Experience Company? Take their Euro-shilling
And spend long starless midnight hours just filling
Screen after screen with longish lines and shorter,
Counting up to a thousand? Intrigued, I bought a
Copy to read it on a Balkan train . . .

I was en route for Târgu Mureş. Not
A bad choice, the book seemed at a first look,
When I found a seat after Miercurea Ciuc.
Yet the reason why much in-your-face poetry
Doesn't appeal to veteran lags like me
Is not its vein of brutal emphasis,
But that its custard pies too often miss
– Unlike the young man in the busy station
At Sfântu Gheorghe where, to the consternation
Of the other passengers he took a leap
At a train as it gathered speed, didn't keep
An eye out for footholds, managed to get
His hands on two bars at shoulder level, set
His left foot to find the carriage step – and failed,
Looked as if he would fall. Gypsy girls wailed
In horror, thinking they'd see him carried

Under the train, and mutilated ('Married,
With two young children, Mr Nagy Bela,
Whose friends said he could be "a daring feller,
But too rash sometimes", died of the injuries
To his back and hips, his ankles and his knees
He suffered trying to jump a moving train,'
The newspaper would say.) Then we saw him gain
The merest toe-grip on the metal ledge
Under the carriage door, and on the edge
Of catastrophe drew back, all in a second
Turning away from where his death had beckoned,
Hauling himself to safety.

                                  So what's it for,
This long sub-Virgilian metaphor
Derived from what I'd witnessed? Undertaking
To chart a year in verse resembles making
A dash at a moving train to get a hold
On something solid as it speeds up – bold,
But pretty risky. Though the idea appeals,
You could easily get dragged under the wheels
Of the fastest moving century so far,
And one of the most untidy and bizarre.

Nineteen ninety-nine, one of the worst years yet,
Saw Third World nations stuck in deeper debt
To the IMF, who said, please suffer more.
Until you do, we can't be really sure
That you want to 'modernise', 'reform' and be
Part of the great global economy.
Dams must be built, children must die and thank
The WTO and the World Bank
For the opportunity. Drought and flood
Will decimate with wafting sand and mud
The Sudan and Mozambique; although
We'll splash out cash for bombs on Kosovo,

Belgrade and Novi Sad, oh dear, there's no
Way we can, when it's Africa, fly in
Not cluster bombs, but food and medicine.

Well, then – On your marks, Simon . . . Get set . . . *Go!*

THEORY OF A FATHER

'I can say that Darren has been different
Since he started seeing you,' his father says
To Maria, the Andorran meteo-chick.
'You must not be offended that I first thought
You might not be the best sort of influence.
But he has changed, and it must be due to you.'

Maria nods and smiles. 'I come', she replies,
'From a little-known country to a well-known place.
Your Darren has been a firm location for me,
As I, I venture to think, may have been for him'
(Though that line she does only think, doesn't say out loud)
'And he's passed in all his subjects!'
                                        'Seven A's,'

Replies the father, 'and one B which I believe
By rights should have been an A. In geography,
Which is his best subject. We shall appeal,
As you might expect'. And then he leaves
A very slight pause before he says, 'I notice
You are pregnant, by the way. The change of climate?'

SATURDAY AFTERNOON

The helicopter stuck like a trapped fly
In desperate buzzing circles, every eye
In Hampstead High Street wondering exactly
What it was doing. Tersely, matter-of-factly,
A young man I asked said there had just now been
'Two guys raiding the chemist's – they've been seen
And reported via 999. They ran
Into the flats behind the Everyman'
– Where, indeed, five white police cars flashing lights
Are drawn up in the cul-de-sac. Such sights
Seem more connected with a larger sin
Than nicking aspirin or shampoo, and in
Our crazed and fathomless world, who knows
Precisely what transgression meant that those
'Resources were deployed', and at what cost?
What had the chemist actually lost
To justify those forces? What dark potion,
Lethal or psychedelic, caused a commotion
Bringing half Hampstead to a sudden stop
To catch two raiders running from a shop?
Shake the kaleidoscope: all goods mean crime,
And shape a different pattern every time.

UP THERE

He could not help seeing their love as like
Two solid-seeming clouds that had blended too suddenly

And left only other people's unsure recall
Of the shapes they had seen in their sky some moments before.

How can two confections of mist unlock themselves
And be distinct again? And live on like that?

And if that is possible, how to require all those others
To see them as separate? As if they had not been one?

TEN RIFFS FOR 2001

(for John Mole at sixty)

Don't chew it tOo much after dusk, thEn it'S in with a chance

the ambient bedroom: air condiTioning braces, storage Heating relaxes. Choose a brand that adapts to eithEr option

but order another as insurance: Sign here, Please tick the box bElow if you wish your signAture not to be foRged for all purchases Made In the new millenNium (visit our websiTe)

in the night, dreaming is beLieving! All yOur friendS are flExible

commercial: 'taste ours by e-maIl' . . . (but remember, 'e' sTands for exceSs)

'your Future without some? Like a tate modern full of bAseball caps who drink from Vast bOttles of water, and talk Unaware into mobiles for eveR'

the small hOurs . . . dark Night of the soul in sugar-free withdrawal . . .

except, well, The tecHnology might be hElpful –

BelievE me, its wonDers surPass belief. You could recOnstitute the original from Some dna lefT on that brass ball . . .

and on the horizOn at dawn, isn't that a Virtual unchEwed fResh pastille? An oblong of oNgoing lIfe standinG by to Help if all opTimism fails?

PAROLE

(i.m. I. H.)

The lately dead still arrive in the corner of your eye
Past the restaurant window, preparing slow smiles of pride
At achieving their return. They know that without them
You can never be the same, so they cheat for a while.
They keep trying to work a parole to the usual places,
They won't be excluded from them if you are there.

Their fingers have pressed the latch and the door nearly opens,
But then their smile turns embarrassed because they find
It behaves like a turnstile: they think they have admission,
But this door is fixed to prevent them coming back in.
And you just can't help, at all; if you went out to greet them
They would not be there, no one in the street would have seen
     them.

Then slowly the corner of your eye
Forgets to look.

Suddenly into the hugeness of the Tourist Hotel
Arrive three-hundred-and-twenty archaeologists,
The Annual National Archaeological Congress.

                                                  At breakfast,

I ask in faltering parody of their language,
'Why are you here?' 'To excavate an ancient historical site,'
Is the reply of the man whose badge reveals
He is 'Professor Szkrvzc'.

                                 One local paper
Writes with a similar message. The other rag,
The organ of the other ethnicity,
Says, 'That's a lie, faithful readers. They are here
In an arrantly dishonest endeavour to prove
That this terrain was, in the earliest times, the home
Of the ancestors of the present minority,
Who thus can claim it as theirs, old pots and sherds
Will show it beyond doubt, that's what they hope . . .'

I ask no more questions of individuals,
But next day go and stand in unseasonal rain,
And watch the insistent digging going on
In the search for ancient tools and artefacts
Made with much more desire to cultivate, and eat,
Than to validate future boundaries,
And watch their eyes as they prise away hard clay
From potentially momentous bits and pieces,
Or just other hunks of harder ancient clay,
And listen in case there are sudden cheers (which there aren't)
At discovering something wonderful which provides
A much-desired political revelation

– And recall the words Albert Camus used in
A story I used to read to grammar school boys
Fifty years ago, before the latest troubles,

Though long after Hamlet's father and the Polacks
Went out on the frozen wastes to smite each other,
With many articulate sons dead because of that:
Camus on the 'rotten spite, the tireless hates,
The blood lust of all men'.

AT NATALIE'S

An arm reached round a shoulder and not removed,
A long kiss taken freely on closed lips
– She knew they meant much more than two feet spread
Three feet apart at the end of a kitchen roll.

So this was the convention enforced at Natalie's:
All tenderness was forbidden, act or word.
It couldn't be listed, priced, or done with screams
For extra payment, topless or quite stark.

It meant real names, and meetings out of bounds.
It did not go with her pictures, rugs, or lamps . . .
It was such innocence, such wasted energy . . .
She required it to be as rare there as anywhere.

ENTERTAINMENTS

Here's the TV and here's the handset lying
Alongside . . . After half-an-hour defying
My techno-incapacity, I can show
Anyone how to work this, how to go
Through the different recondite symbols on
The buttons, and get it working. – And there's one
Hell of a girl on! Stripping to next-to-nothing
As a band plays a tripping little theme. In a sing-

song voice she says Thank you, *thank you*, for the applause.
Then a boy brings a basket, there's a short pause
While she takes the lid off and dips a hand inside
To produce her accomplice, which has tried
Not to get involved, but . . . This big tabby cat
She sets on a step-ladder, gives a gentle pat
To its furry finale – And look! It doesn't stop
Until it's climbed up to the very top,

Where it perches – and leaps safely into her arms.
None of this folly actually harms
The cat, its owner, the manager, or the audience
– Which then claps again – but the whole experience
Leaves me concerned about the small extra ozone gap
It tears out of the already mottled map
Of the atmosphere of consciousness . . .
                                        How I feel the lack
Of old maypoles, just to dance round. Bring them back.

BRAZIER

We have brought out the brazier because the brute
   Heads are hectoring again,
And the rat-eyes in the heads are re-checking old reels
   For invidious information.

Small brains behind the eyes are trying to find
   Grey traces of the faces
In the crowd that created confusion during that last
   – Inconclusive – confrontation.

The money behind the memory tracking the moment
   Recorded on audio
When conniving voices were caught in the corridor after
   That 'deplorable demonstration'

Has paid for the dismal devices designed
   To nest in walls neatly,
And listen, and for the CC equipment eyeing
   Long delays over defecation

In the interim. Touch these inserted instruments
   If you could, they would be cold.
Touch the brazier with brute money, take your hand
   Back in consternation.

A tannoy is bellowing bald and brutal advice:
   'Damp the brazier down,
Save your jobs, save your families, save the nation.
   Stay in negotiation.'

– 'What? Get ripped off, and hassled and harried?
   Left stranded, and empty-handed,
And nearly run down on the line? That's fine!
   That's some salvation!'

'Our brazier settles and glows as the drear day darkens.
  Come over and open your own
Empty hands, warm them, feel the strength of fire
  In its proper station.'